THE Teapot TRAIL

RECIPE BOOK

SERIES II

THE IDEAL COMPANION TO THE
ORIGINAL TEAPOT TRAIL RECIPE BOOK, VOLUME I

Introduction

One town centre looks very much like another these days, with a depressingly uniform array of snack bars and cafés. It makes a refreshing change, then, to find tea-rooms where eating is still regarded as a pleasure rather than a chore, where quality teas and coffees and home-baked cakes can be savoured in congenial surroundings.

If you have enjoyed visiting the tea-rooms featured in the Original Teapot Trail Series, and long to taste the delicious fare again, then this recipe book is just for you. For each recipe comes from one of our selected establishments, where it is a regular feature on the menu. Try you hand at Pork and Cider Cobbler from Somerset, Lavender Biscuits from Norfolk, Dorset Apple Cake, Banana Cake from Norfolk, Prawn and Haddock Bake from Sussex.

You'll find recipes for soups, snacks and main meals as well as the puddings, cakes and pastries that are essential to any traditional tea-room. So set out your best china, brew a good pot of tea and introduce your family and friends to the pleasures of The Teapot Trail.

Caroline Alderson.

Contents

Introduction   1

Soups & Starters

Cauliflower & Stilton Soup   3
Courgette & Cumin Soup   3
Parsnip & Apple Soup   4
Cheese Stuffed Mushrooms   4
Country Vegetable Soup   5
Tomato & Mint Soup   5
Carrot & Orange Soup   6
Kipper Pâté   6
Walnut & Mushroom Soup   7
Chicken Liver Pâté   7

Savoury Snacks

Tuna & Pasta Salad   8
Wiltshire Bacon Scones   9
Cheese Strata   9
Somerset Cheese Scones   10
Salmon & Cheese Flan   10

Main Meals

Pork in Orange Sauce   11
Savoury Stuffed Peppers   11
Game "Two" Casserole   12
Mushroom & Walnut Stroganoff   12
Chicken & Broccoli Bake   13
Tender Braised Lamb with Apricots
& Almonds   13
Lamb Chops Patrick   14
Sweet & Sour Chicken   14
Blacksmiths Steak Pie   15
Kitchen Garden Vegetable Hot Pot   15
Prawn & Haddock Bake   16
Mushrooms & Bacon in Red Wine   16

Teatime Treats

Gooseberry & Orange Jam   17
Carrot & Walnut Cake   17
Lavender Biscuits   18
Orange & Apricot Squares   18
Norton House Home-made Rock Cakes   19
Cherry & Almond Slice   19
Sultana Flapjack   20
Fudge Chocolate Cake   20
Caraway Seed Cake   20
Barton Chocolate Bar   21
Norfolk Shortcakes   21
Chocolate Brownies   22
Frome Fairings   22
Sticky Gingerbread   23
Banana Cake   23
Coconut Cake   23
Apricot Slices   24
Caribbean Fruit Cake   24
Orange Chocolate Drizzle Cake   25
Dorset Apple Cake   25
Bienenstick   26
Boiled Fruit Cake   26

Tarts & Puddings

Christmas Pudding   27
18th-Century Lemon Cheese Cake   28
Caribbean Bakewell   28
French Apple Flan   29
Apricot & Maple Syrup Pudding   29
Bread Pudding   30
Fruit Tartlet   30
Old Thatch Carrot Cake   31
Butterscotch Meringue Pie   31
Mrs Jones' Rich Rice Pudding   32
Hungarian Nut Torte   32

C.P. Printing & Publishing Ltd. wish to thank the many tea-shop proprietors from the Yorkshire Wolds, Hereford & Worcestershire, Shropshire, Norfolk, Suffolk, Somerset, Dorset, Sussex, Gloucestershire & the Cotswolds, Hampshire & the Isle of Wight, Wiltshire & Avon and Shakespeare Country (Oxfordshire and Warwickshire) who have contributed their favourite recipes to this publication. You will find further details of these tea-shops in the successful Teapot Trail series, listed at the back. Special thanks go to Polly Collins and Chris Heard, proprietors of Glebe Cottage tea-room in Kildale near Whitby, for their help in checking the recipes.

Cauliflower & Stilton Soup

Just off the A27, between Firle and Selmeston is East Sussex, lies Middle Farm, the "English Farm Cider Centre". Here you'll find the largest gathering of real farmhouse ciders and perries in the country (more than 150 varieties!) as well as organic fruit and vegetables in the Farm Shop and over 70 English cheeses! Only the best Stilton goes into this tasty, wholesome soup — a regular favourite in the converted barn tea-shop.

1 medium sized cauliflower (chopped) *4oz (110g) Stilton cheese*
1 medium onion (chopped) *½pt (275ml) milk*
1 medium potato (chopped) *1oz (25g) margarine*
½pt (275ml) seasoned stock *cream (optional)*

1. Melt the margarine in a large pan and add onions to soften. Add chopped cauliflower, potato and stock. Cook until vegetables are just tender.
2. Transfer mixture into a liquidizer and purée.
3. Crumble Stilton and stir in until dissolved. Add milk and a little cream if desired.
4. Reheat and serve with parsley garnish. *(Serves 4)*

Courgette & Cumin Soup

The little market town of Framlingham, Suffolk, is well known for its magnificent castle site. Lovers of fine food also know it as the home of Teapots and Quails, just off the market place opposite the church. Here, Pru Gibbons and Lesley Holloway specialise in unusual soups such as this popular recipe, simple but excellent.

1oz (25g) butter *12oz (350g) courgettes, sliced thickly*
1 onion, chopped *(reserve a few thin slices for garnish)*
1 clove garlic, crushed *¾pt (425ml) chicken or vegetable stock*
1 level tsp. cumin *½pt (275ml) milk*
5oz (150g) potato, diced *salt and freshly ground pepper*

1. Melt the butter in a large pan and gently fry the chopped onion and crushed garlic until soft. Add the cumin and cook for 2-3 minutes.
2. Add the diced potato, sliced courgette and stock and cook until the vegetables are tender.
3. Liquidize the mixture and return to the pan. Add the ground pepper and salt if required.
4. Add the milk and heat through (do not boil). Serve and garnish with sliced courgette. *Serves 4.*

Parsnip and Apple Soup

At Mangerton, near Bridport, lies one of Dorset's gems — the 17th century Mangerton Mill. Complete with working millwheel, by-gones museum and trout lake, a tour round the mill is an experience not to be missed. In the low-beamed tea-room, Ruth Harris and daughter-in-law Hazel often serve this rich, creamy textured soup — wonderfully warming on a chilly day.

1oz (25g) butter
1½lb (700g) parsnips, peeled and
chopped
1 Bramley cooking apple, peeled and
chopped

2 pints chicken stock
½ tsp dried sage
2 cloves
5 fl oz (¼pt) single cream
salt and pepper

1. Melt the butter in a large saucepan. Add the parsnips and apple, then cover and cook gently for 10 minutes, stirring occasionally.
2. Add the stock, sage and cloves. Bring to the boil, cover and simmer for 30 minutes.
3. Remove the cloves, leave to cool slightly then purée in a blender.
4. Return to the saucepan and reheat gently with the cream. Season to taste.
5. Serve hot, garnished with croûtons or parsley. *Serves 6-8.*

Cheese Stuffed Mushrooms

"Merely to walk down its long street is a recipe for happiness". So noted one visitor to Chipping Campden, in the heart of the Cotswolds. Just set back from the 17th century Market Hall, with its splendid arches, stands the Cotswold House Hotel — a charming, traditional hotel whose attractions have been increased by the addition of Greenstocks, a combination of bistro, wine-bar and tea-shop. This recipe, although quite rich, has been very popular ever since it was invented in 1977.

20 medium sized mushrooms
12oz (350g) grated Cheddar cheese
1 heaped tsp. finely grated onion

1 level tsp. curry powder
2-3 tbsp. mayonnaise
freshly ground black pepper

1. Remove mushroom stalks and place caps upside down in an ovenproof dish.
2. Combine remaining ingredients and use this mixture to stuff the mushrooms.
3. Place mushrooms in a pre-heated oven (400°F/200°C/gas 6) for 10 minutes, until mixture is bubbling. They can be transferred to a hot grill to brown them but this is not essential.
4. Serve immediately, with fresh granary bread to mop up the juices. *Serves 4.*

Country Vegetable Soup

As you drive up the A33 north-east of Basingstoke, look out for signs to Hartley's Tea Room at Sherfield on Loddon, located within a garden centre complex. Sarah Mott is renowned for her soups, beautifully presented in covered china bowls. You can use any vegetables in this versatile country vegetable soup, and any combination of fresh herbs — depending on what's available in the garden. You will need approximately 2½lbs. of vegetables to 2½ pints of water.

1 medium onion
3 medium carrots
1 small parsnip
1 small swede
2 medium potatoes
2oz (50g) red lentils
any other vegetables according to season

1 level tsp. mixed dried herbs
2½-3 pints of water
freshly chopped chives or parsley — for serving
salt and pepper to taste
2 or 3 tbsp. fresh cream (optional)

1. Peel and roughly chop vegetables and place in a large saucepan.
2. Cover vegetables with water, add lentils and herbs and bring to the boil.
3. Cover and simmer for 30-40 minutes until vegetables are tender. Add salt and pepper to taste. Fresh cream can be added for extra richness.
4. Garnish with chopped chives or parsley and serve. *Serves 6.*

Tomato & Mint Soup

Chris Bland, proprietor of the Acorn Wholefood Restaurant and Coffee House in Church Stretton, Shropshire, specialises in soups that are a little out of the ordinary. When tomatoes are plentiful in summer and early autumn, the combination of flavours is both tasty and refreshing.

1lb (450g) fresh tomatoes, skinned and chopped
2 tbsp. tomato purée
1 tsp. demerara sugar
2 medium onions
1 oz (25g) fresh mint (or more, if preferred)

1 tbsp. sunflower or olive oil
¾ pt (425ml) vegetable stock
salt & black pepper
1 clove garlic, crushed
dash of lemon juice

1. Chop the onions and sautée in hot oil with the crushed garlic.
2. Add the chopped, skinned tomatoes and chopped mint and simmer for 15 minutes.
3. Add tomato purée, seasoning, stock, sugar and lemon juice and simmer for a further 15 minutes.
4. Serve with a swirl of yoghurt and fresh chopped mint — delicious!

Carrot & Orange Soup

From the Ombersley Gallery Restaurant and Tea Room, just 4 miles west of Droitwich Spa, comes this imaginative, tangy soup — an unusual start to any meal, delicious served with warm, crusty bread!

1oz (25g) butter
1 tbsp oil
1lb (450g) carrots — sliced
2 med. onions — chopped

¾oz (20g) plain flour
1½pts (850ml) chicken stock
½ grated rind and juice of one orange
salt and pepper to taste

1. Heat the butter and oil in a saucepan and add the carrot and onion. Fry until soft.
2. Sprinkle in the flour and cook, stirring, for 1 minute.
3. Remove from heat and gradually stir in the stock.
4. Return to the heat and bring to the boil, stirring. Add the orange juice and rind, plus salt and pepper.
5. Cover and simmer for 30 minutes.
6. Cool slightly then place into an electric blender and blend until smooth.

Kipper Pâté

Madresfield is a tiny hamlet 1½ miles east of Malvern, in the heart of Worcestershire. It centres on Madresfield Court, a moated Tudor house owned by the Lygon family since about 1160. The Lygon's Victorian walled kitchen garden was restored in 1987 by Ron and Margery Bithell, along with daughter Hilary and her husband Stephen Collins. It now provides the perfect setting for a garden centre and Humphrey's tea-room, where this simple but delicious pâté (Hilary's favourite) is much in demand.

2 boned kippers (1 pack frozen)
2tbsp. greek yoghurt
3oz (75g) unsalted butter (softened)

1tbsp lemon juice
cayenne pepper
¼tsp. ground mace

1. Cook kippers — as per instructions on pack if frozen, or place on a plate, cover and microwave on high for 2 minutes. Allow to cool a little.
2. Remove skins and any larger bones.
3. Blend kippers, butter and greek yoghurt together. Add cayenne pepper, lemon juice and mace. Mix again.
4. Put into ramekins and refridgerate until firm.
5. Garnish with thin lemon slices.

NOTE: Can be frozen. To defrost, leave overnight in fridge or in microwave — 3 minutes on defrost. *Serves 4.*

Walnut & Mushroom Soup

The pretty little town of Cleobury Mortimer, east of Ludlow, stands on a hillside running down to a wide sweep of the river Rea. At the top of the High Street, The Tea Room and Card Shop provides delicious home-made refreshment, created by proprietor Anne Mathews. This light, tasty soup is best made with the dark, flat mushrooms which have more flavour than the closed button variety.

1lb (450g) mushrooms
1 medium sized onion, skinned and chopped
2oz (50g) butter
1 tbsp. flour
1 pint (570ml) chicken stock

1 pint (570ml) milk
2oz (50g) walnuts, chopped
½ tsp. salt
freshly ground pepper
5 fl oz (¼ pint) single cream

1. Wipe and chop mushrooms, reserving a few finely sliced mushrooms for garnish.
2. Melt the butter in a saucepan and fry the onions until softened. Add the chopped mushrooms and cook for 2 minutes.
3. Remove from the heat, stir in flour, stock, milk, walnuts and seasoning. Bring to the boil. Cover and simmer for ½ hour.
4. Purée the soup, add reserved mushrooms and cream, return to the pan and cook slowly for approximately 5 minutes. Do not boil. Serve hot with fresh, crusty bread.

Chicken Liver Pâté

Right on the A1067 Norwich to Fakenham road in Great Witchingham you'll find Ken and Sue Maxim's small but friendly tea-room and craft shop — "Maxim's". Browse round the wide selection of local, British and overseas crafts and enjoy some of the delicious home-cooked cakes, lunches and snacks. Sue serves this tasty pâté with huge chunks of wholemeal bread, pickles and salad — a meal in itself!

2oz (50g) margarine
1 large onion (peeled and finely chopped)
8oz (225g) chicken livers (sliced, chopped and grisly bits removed)

1 tsp. dried thyme
salt and ground pepper
2 bay leaves
½ tbsp. sherry

1. Heat margarine and fry onions for a few minutes until soft.
2. Add the chicken livers, thyme, seasoning and bay leaves and cook thoroughly for at least 5 minutes (until there are no pink tinges).
3. Allow to cool slightly, remove bay leaves.
4. Pour into a liquidiser with the sherry and purée to a cream.
5. Spoon into individual ramekins, cover with cling film and refridgerate to harden. *Makes 4 ramekins.*

Tuna & Pasta Salad

Set on the eastern fringes of the Yorkshire Wolds, just 2½ miles from Filey and the Yorkshire Coast, the village of Hunmanby is a tranquil spot, its fine old main street flanked by whitewashed cottages and characterful pubs. For many people the main attraction here is Walkers of Hunmanby, run by Jenny and Terry Walker as a quality delicatessen and tea-room. This salad is on sale in the delicatessen and is served with salads in the tea-room — delicious hot or cold and simple to prepare.

1 x 7oz tin tuna in oil
4oz (110g) pasta shells or twists, cooked
1 tbsp. olive oil
½ small green pepper, de-seeded and
chopped

2 tomatoes, chopped
1 tbsp. cooked peas
1 tbsp. cooked sweetcorn
small stick celery, chopped
1 garlic clove, finely chopped

Ensure all ingredients are cold before mixing them together, then serve on a bed of lettuce with a crusty roll and butter.

Alternatively, this recipe is delicious mixed when the ingredients are still warm, and served in a tomato sauce.

TOMATO SAUCE
1 x 14oz tin chopped tomatoes
1 medium onion
2 tbsp. tomato purée

½ tsp. Italian mixed herbs
a little oil for frying
1 garlic clove

1. Finely chop garlic and onion and fry gently for 5 minutes until soft, but not brown.
2. Add other ingredients and simmer gently until the sauce has thickened (approx. 15-20 minutes), stirring occasionally.
3. Serve immediately on tuna and pasta dish.

Wiltshire Bacon Scones

The little village of Zeals, on the Wiltshire/Dorset/Somerset border, is best known as the home of Stag Cottage Tea Room, where Marie and Peter Boxall have been welcoming hungry visitors for many years. Scones are Marie's speciality and this county recipe is popular at any time of day.

8oz (225g) self-raising flour
2oz (50g) butter or margarine
2oz (50g) grated cheese
2oz (50g) lightly cooked bacon, finely chopped

¼pt (150ml) milk - fresh or dried
1tbsp tomato ketchup
1 tsp Worcester sauce
salt and pepper to taste

1. Pre-heat the oven to 200°C/400°F/gas mark 6.
2. Rub the fat into the flour until the mixture resembles breadcrumbs, then add the cheese and bacon.
3. Add the sauces and seasoning to the milk (if using dried milk, beat the powder into the water to make ¼pt). Add to the flour mixture to make a stiff dough.
4. Roll out the dough lightly on a floured board to ¾″ thickness. Cut out the scones with a 2″ square cutter.
5. Brush the tops with beaten egg or dust with flour, place on a greased baking tray and bake for approximately 15 minutes until they are a golden brown.

Cheese Strata

Bridgnorth in Shropshire holds a number of surprises. The Town Hall arches over half the High Street and still shelters the stalls of the Saturday market, while the Castle Hill Railway is Britain's sole surviving inland cliff railway. Whitburn Coffee House in Whitburn Street holds a few surprises too — maybe a folk band on a Saturday — but always some delicious culinary treats such as Gaenor Joyce's Cheese Strata or Pudding, a variation of the traditional quiche.

4oz (110g) diced bacon
1tsp. oil
1 chopped onion
butter (or low fat spread)
5 slices bread (brown adds more flavour)

6oz (175g) grated Cheddar
4 eggs (beaten lightly)
¾pt single cream
¼tsp. paprika
¼tsp. chilli powder
1tsp. mustard (wholegrain)

1. Fry bacon until crisp in oil and then drain.
2. Fry onion in same pan until soft and drain.
3. Butter bread and cut into cubes.
4. Line a 9″ diameter deep flan dish with half of the bread. Sprinkle half the cheese on top.
5. Add the rest of the bread and remaining cheese. Scatter bacon and onions on top.
6. Beat together the eggs, cream, mustard and spices and pour over the top.
7. Refrigerate for at least 8 hours.
8. Bake in oven for 1 hour at gas 3, 170°C, 375°F.
9. Slice and serve with a fresh mixed salad. *4 very generous portions.*

Somerset Cheese Scones

Bypassed by the A39 to the north-west of Bridgwater, the little village of Nether Stowey has changed little since the days when Samuel Taylor Coleridge wrote his famous Rime of the Ancient Mariner here. The timeless feel is reinforced when you enter the 300-year-old Castle Cottage Tea Room, where Alec Mortimer creates delicious daily specials, soups, and mouth-watering light cakes and scones.

13oz (375g) Self Raising flour
3fl oz sunflower oil
3fl oz milk
3fl oz water
1 large egg (free range)

4oz (110g) Cheddar cheese (mature if possible), grated
1 tsp. mustard
½ tsp. salt
½ tsp. baking powder

1. Mix all the dry ingredients together.
2. Whisk the egg, milk, water and oil together and gradually add to the dry ingredients until you have a soft, pliable dough.
3. Roll out the dough on a floured board to ½″ thickness and cut into circles. Place on a lightly greased baking tray and glaze with milk or any remaining egg/water/oil/milk mixture.
4. Bake in the oven at gas mark 7/220°C/425°F for 15 minutes until they are a light golden brown on top.

Delicious served warm, oozing with butter! (Makes 13-14 scones).

Salmon & Cheese Flan

From The Courtyard Centre near Lytchett Minster in Dorset comes this tasty quiche, ideal for light lunches and high teas — one of Linda Wise's speciality dishes in Dylan's Tea Room.

8oz (225g) shortcrust pastry
1 large beaten egg
¼pt. (150ml) of milk
3oz (75g) grated onion
salt and pepper

7½oz canned pink salmon
4oz (110g) grated cheese
pinch of nutmeg
cucumber, for garnish

1. Grease an 8″ flan dish and place on a baking sheet. Roll out pastry and line dish. Prick the base all over using a fork.
2. Whisk together the egg and milk.
3. Place the grated onion in the bottom of the pastry case.
4. Drain the salmon and discard any dark skin or bone. Flake the fish and spoon over the onions in the pastry case.
5. Pour over the egg mix, and season with salt and pepper.
6. Scatter grated cheese over the mix, and gently sprinkle with a little fresh nutmeg. Cook gently in the centre of the oven, 400°F/200°C or gas mark 6, for about 20 minutes. Reduce heat to 350°F/180°C or gas mark 4, for a further 25 minutes, until golden brown and set.

Main Meals

Pork in Orange Sauce

The delightful village of Chawton, near Alton in Hampshire, is famous throughout the world. A place of pilgrimage for devotees of Jane Austen, who lived here and wrote or revised her six great novels, from 1809 to 1817. You can visit her 17th century home with its garden of old-fashioned flowers, then cross the road to Cassandras Cup, an equally delightful tea-room run by Michael and Ena Goodman, where this tangy pork dish is always a popular feature on the daily specials board.

3lb (1kg 350g) cubed pork
1oz (25g) butter
1oz (25g) flour
salt & pepper

2 tsp. mixed herbs
little garlic to taste
250ml orange juice

1. Salt and pepper the pork and cover with flour.
2. Melt butter in frying pan, add pork to pan and sauté until lightly brown.
3. Add garlic and mixed herbs.
4. Place pork in ovenproof dish, add the orange juice and cover with a lid.
5. Cook slowly for 1½ hours on gas 5/190°C/275°F.
6. Serve on a bed of rice, decorated with a slice of fresh orange. *Serves 6.*

Savoury Stuffed Peppers

Storrington: a small Sussex town with an unassuming old church, swans drifting across a picturesque pond fringed by weeping willow trees, and beside the pond, an English country garden and tea-shop — what more could anyone ask for? David and Nicole Weston are both esthusiastic and adventurous cooks, and there's plenty to tempt on the menu at the Willow Tea Room. This daily special is delicious served on a bed of rice.

4 medium, de-seeded green peppers
4 courgettes, sliced
14oz tin tomatoes
1 aubergine, chopped
1 tsp. mixed herbs

1½ onions, chopped
2tbs. olive oil
1 tsp. tomato purée
pinch of salt and pepper

FOR THE STUFFING
1oz (25g) brown rice
6oz (175g) ground lean beef
6oz (175g) ground lean pork
½ onion, chopped

1 tsp. mixed herbs
1 egg
pinch of salt & pepper

1. Make the stuffing. Mix the 1oz. of rice, ½ chopped onion, 6oz. each of ground beef and pork, mixed herbs, egg, salt and pepper and stuff an equal amount into the prepared green peppers.
2. Heat the olive oil in a heavy based casserole or saucepan and sautée the rest of the chopped onions until lightly cooked.
3. Add the 4 stuffed peppers, sliced courgettes, aubergine, tomatoes, tomato purée, mixed herbs, salt and pepper and bring to the boil.
4. Lightly simmer for approximately ¾ hour or until the peppers are cooked.

Game "Two" Casserole

The attractive Cotswold town of Chipping Norton is home to the Market House restaurant and guest house. Jan Meek and her daughter Becky do all the cooking and this tasty, economical recipe is a popular "special" — an excellent way of using up what remains of a brace of pheasant. (Jan tends to freeze them after the "first" time of eating, and bring them out at a later date).

FOR THE STOCK
The cooked carcasses of two pheasant
one onion, chopped
2 carrots, chopped
bay leaf
bouquet garni
water

FOR THE MAIN DISH
larger pieces of meat from the carcasses
2 large onions, thinly sliced and cooked until soft
8 rashers of back bacon, cut into pieces
1 Savoy cabbage torn roughly into pieces
8 juniper berries (crushed)

1. Make the stock. Boil the 2 pheasant carcasses (in sufficient water to cover) with chopped onion, carrots, a bay leaf and bouquet garni for 1½-2 hours to make a rich stock.
2. Butter the base of a casserole dish. Arrange the onions, bacon, cabbage and pieces of meat in alternate layers, finishing with a layer of bacon.
3. Pour the stock into the casserole dish until it nearly reaches the top.
4. Scatter the crushed juniper berries on top, cover and cook at gas mark 4/350°F/180°C for 2-3 hours. 20 minutes before the end of cooking time, remove the lid to let the bacon brown a little.

Mushroom & Walnut Stroganoff
(Use Organic ingredients where available)

The tiny village of Ryton-on-Dunsmore, near Coventry, is home to the Ryton Organic Gardens, featured on the Channel 4 TV series "All Muck and Magic." Alan and Jackie Gear provide the most welcoming and comprehensive survey of organic gardening in Europe and a tea-shop and restaurant offering the very best of organically-grown food.

3lb (1.4kg) button mushrooms
8oz (250g) chopped walnuts
2oz (50g) butter
2tbsp (30ml) light olive oil
1 onion, finely chopped
1 garlic clove, crushed
3½fl oz (100ml) dry white wine (optional)
1tbsp (15ml) wholemeal flour
½pt (300ml) single cream
squeeze of lemon juice
sea salt and freshly ground black pepper

1. Wash the mushrooms, pat dry on absorbent kitchen paper, then slice thickly. Heat the butter and oil together in a large heavy-based pan. Add the onions and garlic, cover and cook gently for about 10 minutes until softened.
2. Add the mushrooms and walnuts, stir well and cook for 20-30 minutes until all the excess liquid has evaporated. Pour in the wine if using and let it bubble down until only a few spoonfuls of liquid remain.
3. Blend the wholemeal flour with a little of the cream until smooth, then stir into the mushrooms with the rest of the cream. Slowly bring to the boil, stirring, and simmer for 2-3 minutes until thickened.
4. Remove from the heat and stir in lemon juice, salt and pepper to taste. Serve immediately, with rice. *Serves 6.*

Chicken & Broccoli Bake

The enchanting little town of Winchcombe in the Cotswolds has been welcoming pilgrims for centuries to its Abbey and nearby Sudeley Castle. Visitors today find a particularly warm welcome at The Olde Bakery Tea Shoppe in the High Street, where Colin and Sally Snell have built up an excellent reputation for quality home-cooked food.

cooked meat from ½ a 4lb chicken
1 good sized head of broccoli

3oz (75g) fresh breadcrumbs

FOR CHEESE SAUCE
½pt (275ml) milk
2oz (50g) butter

1 tbsp. of flour
6oz (175g) grated cheese

1. Cut up the cooked chicken into bite-size pieces and place in an ovenproof dish. Cook broccoli for 10 minutes approximately, drain and place in dish with chicken.
2. Make the sauce. Melt the butter in a saucepan. Remove from the heat and add the flour.
3. Gradually add the milk, return to the heat and keep stirring slowly until the sauce is smooth.
4. Add the cheese and stir for a further 5 minutes. Add salt and pepper to taste and pour the sauce over the chicken and broccoli.
5. Finally sprinkle breadcrumbs over the dish and place in a pre-heated oven on gas mark 4/180°C/350°F for 20-30 minutes until golden brown.
6. Serve with fresh vegetables. *Serves 4.*

Tender Braised Lamb with Apricots & Almonds

Wholesome and thoroughly delicious, this lamb dish flavoured with rosemary and apricots goes well with rice and a simple green salad. Just one of the imaginative dishes on offer at the Flora Twort Gallery and Restaurant in Petersfield, Hampshire, run by Gaye and Richard Bartlett.

1lb 2oz (500g) lean diced lamb
1oz (25g) margarine or oil
1 medium onion — chopped
1 stick celery — chopped
1oz (25g) mushrooms — sliced
1oz (25g) plain flour
1 tbsp. tomato purée

1 pint (570ml) brown stock
1 bouquet garni
1 small sprig fresh rosemary
1 tin apricots — strained
1oz (25g) toasted flaked almonds
parsley to garnish

1. Fry the meat in the oil to seal it (just enough to brown the outside).
2. Add the vegetables and continue cooking.
3. Add the flour and allow to cook for a few moments.
4. Add the tomato purée and then gradually add the stock.
5. Add the bouquet garni and rosemary and simmer until cooked (approx. 1-2 hours).
6. Add the drained apricots and simmer for a further 5 minutes. Remove the bouquet garni.
7. Serve sprinkled with the toasted almonds and parsley. *Serves 4.*

Lamb Chops Patrick

The ancient town of Mere in Wiltshire is delightfully peaceful — a charming mixture of architectural styles from the medieval through to the Georgian. Near the Clock Tower you'll find the Welcome House tea-room, restaurant and guest house, where Philip Luckham and Patrick Deering offer a mouthwatering menu that combines the best of British fare with delicacies of their own devising.

DRESSING
1tsp runny honey
5 fl oz mayonnaise

1tsp chopped mint
seasoning

FOR THE LAMB
2 chops per person
2oz (50g) butter
4fl oz (110ml) port
4fl oz (110ml) water

1 clove garlic
2tsp plain flour
2tsp redcurrant jelly
seasoning

1. Prepare the dressing by stirring the honey, mayonnaise and chopped mint (in season) together, season then cover and refrigerate until required.
2. Rub the garlic over the inside of a frying pan, then melt the butter. Fry the lamb chops for 5-8 minutes (according to personal taste), remove and place on a heated plate. Cover and keep warm.
3. Stir the flour into the remaining butter in the pan, then add the port, half the redcurrant jelly and the water, scraping all the meat juices from the base of the pan as you bring the sauce to the boil. Simmer for 2 minutes and season to taste. Pour over the chops and serve.
4. Heat the remaining redcurrant jelly and pour into a little pot. Serve with the dressing as an accompaniment.

Sweet & Sour Chicken

From Somerset's county town of Taunton comes this delicious chicken dish — just one of the daily specials on offer at Number Ten in Station Road.

3lb chicken (boiled), skin & bones removed
2 onions, diced
2 green peppers, diced
1tbsp. oil
½ mug (4oz, 110g) demerara sugar
½ mug (4fl. oz., 110ml) white wine vinegar
1tsp. ginger purée or fresh ground ginger

1 clove garlic, crushed
2 tbsp. tomato purée
approx. 1½pts. (850ml) stock from chicken
salt and pepper
cornflour to thicken
1 tin pineapple chunks
2 dsp. soya sauce

1. Cook the diced onions and peppers in the oil until transparent.
2. Add the sugar, vinegar, ginger, garlic, tomato purée and soya sauce and mix well.
3. Add chicken "stock" from boiled chicken, and season to taste.
4. Simmer for ½ hour. Then thicken with cornflour mixed with a little cold water.
5. Just before serving, add the chicken pieces and pineapple.

Blacksmiths Steak Pie

This appropriately-named dish is a great favourite at The Forge Museum and tea-room in North Creake, Norfolk. The ancient forge is still in use today, run by blacksmith Roy Masters and his wife Barbara, who prepares all the meals, breads and cakes in the adjacent tea-room. She serves this pie as part of the "Blacksmiths Lunch" with salad and delightful horseshoe-shaped bread rolls!

(To make one 8in. plate pie)
SHORTCRUST PASTRY
8oz (225g) Self Raising flour &
pinch of salt
2oz (50g) margarine

2oz (50g) lard
a little water for mixing

FILLING
6oz (175g) beef steak, cubed
2oz (50g) chopped onion
½ tsp. selected home-grown mixed herbs

1pt (570ml) water
2oz (50g) gravy mix
pinch of salt & pepper

1. Place the cubed beef in a heavy pan or flameproof casserole and add the chopped onion, herbs, water and salt and pepper. Cook for approximately ¾ hour, then thicken with the gravy mix.
2. Make the pastry. Rub margarine and lard into the flour until the mixture resembles fine breadcrumbs.
3. Add a little water and mould into a ball.
4. Take half the pastry and line the pie plate with it. Pour in the meat filling, roll out the remainder of the pastry and cover the pie.
5. Brush the pie with egg and bake in the oven at gas mark 6, 400°F, 200°C for approximately 30 minutes or until the pastry is golden and crusty.
6. Serve with simple green salad and crusty bread. *Serves 6.*

Kitchen Garden Vegetable Hot Pot

The Victorian Estate of Oldown is set in beautiful countryside overlooking the River Severn. Developed over the years, it now has a visitor farm where you can feed the animals and milk the cow as well as a thrilling Forest Challenge, pick-your-own fruit and a farm and gift shop. The licensed Kitchen Garden Restaurant is part of the walled garden and uses produce from the garden for this wholesome winter warmer.

1 large onion, peeled and chopped
1 medium swede, peeled and diced
3 medium carrots, peeled and sliced
½ head celery, chopped
4oz (110g) mushrooms, sliced

2 leeks, chopped
large tin (450 grms) tomatoes
1tbsp mixed herbs
2oz (50g) butter
½lb (225g) cheese, grated

1. Melt the butter in a large saucepan. Add the onion, swede, carrots and celery, cover and gently cook for 10 minutes.
2. Add the tomatoes and mixed herbs and cook gently for 20-30 minutes then add the leeks and mushrooms and cook for a further 5 minutes. Check seasoning and add salt and pepper to taste.
3. To serve, place the vegetables and juices in an ovenproof dish, cover with grated cheese and melt under the grill until the cheese is bubbling and golden brown.

Prawn & Haddock Bake

The tiny village of Walberton, near Arundel in Sussex, is home to "Beam Ends" — a delightful thatched 16th century cottage owned by Rick Botteley and Coral Stroud. You can sit in the cosy old tea-room or in the quiet garden with its views across the dene and enjoy traditional cakes and loose-leaf teas as well as daily specials such as this delicious fish dish, which takes about 10 minutes to prepare.

1 large onion, chopped
1 tin Campbells condensed mushroom
soup
2 mushrooms, sliced
4oz (110g) prawns
8oz (225g) pre-cooked haddock fillet

salt and pepper
1 tsp. mixed herbs
4oz (110g) brown breadcrumbs &
2oz (50g) grated cheese, mixed together
a little butter and oil for frying

1. Fry the chopped onion in a little butter and oil until transparent. Add sliced mushrooms and toss for a couple of minutes.
2. Mix the soup in a separate bowl with half a can of water then add to the onions and mushrooms. Lower the heat on the hob and cook gently for a couple of minutes.
3. Add salt and pepper, herbs, flaked, cooked haddock and lastly the prawns.
4. Place the mixture in a fireproof dish and cover generously with the breadcrumbs and grated cheese mixture. Brown for barely one minute under a hot grill.
5. Garnish with a slice of tomato and a sprig of parsley. *Serves 4.*

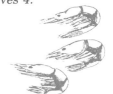

Mushrooms & Bacon in Red Wine

From Emm's Coffee Shop in Wootton Bassett, Wiltshire, comes this delicious recipe which can be used as a starter, main meal or savoury snack. Many of Marilyn Pullen's customers tell her it is an aphrodisiac but this she cannot vouch for — see for yourself!

1lb (450g) fresh field or button
mushrooms
½pt (275ml) good red wine
1tbsp olive oil

4 rashers smoked back bacon
½ onion, peeled and very finely chopped
1tbsp tomato purée
1 bay leaf

1. Wipe clean the mushrooms and slice thickly, but leave whole if button mushrooms are used.
2. Trim the rind and fat from the bacon and slice into thin strips.
3. In a heavy-based saucepan, gently fry the chopped onion in olive oil until soft and transparent. Add the strips of bacon and fry until they are cooked.
4. Pour in the red wine, add the tomato purée and simmer until the mixture thickens.
5. Add the mushrooms and bay leaf and simmer for a further 20 minutes until the mushrooms are al dente (still firm to the bite).
6. Pour the mixture into a heat-proof dish and decorate with sprigs of fresh parsley and triangles of hot granary toast.

Gooseberry & Orange Jam

Just to the north of Leominster in Herefordshire, off the B4362, lies the tiny village of Bircher. Best known to many as the home of Cadwallader Home Farm Tearoom, where Doreen Cadwallader's home-made pies, scones and cakes are served fresh from the oven. Even the jams are home-made, at least 3 varieties on every table. Here is one unusual example to impress your family and friends.

Makes about 2.5kg (5lbs).

3lb (1.5kg) gooseberries
finely grated rind and juice of two
oranges
½pt (300ml) water
3lb (1.5kg) sugar

1. Wash and top and tail the gooseberries and place in a preserving pan.
2. Add the orange rind and juice, together with the water. Simmer gently until fruit is tender.
3. Test for pectin. Remove from heat, add the sugar and stir until dissolved.
4. Return to the heat, bring to the boil and boil rapidly until setting point is reached. (To test for setting point, remove from the heat and spoon a little jam on to a cold saucer and allow to cool. The jam is ready if a skin forms and wrinkles when pushed with a finger).
5. Pour into warmed jars, cover and label.

Carrot & Walnut Cake

The Castle alone makes Warwick an essential stop on any visitor's itinerary, but Warwickshire's county town offers much more. The Old Forge Tea Room in Bowling Green Street for instance, which was a working forge until 1973. Jennifer Downey offers a range of home-baked delights, including this recipe which has many devotees.

7oz (200g) plain flour
6oz (175g) caster sugar
1tsp bicarbonate of soda
1tsp baking powder
½tsp salt
3 eggs
4fl oz (120ml) vegetable oil
½tsp vanilla essence
½tsp cinnamon powder
6oz (175g) grated carrot
2oz (50g) chopped walnuts
3oz (75g) grated apple
3oz (75g) sultanas

FROSTING

2oz (50g) cream cheese
3oz (75g) soft margarine
5oz (125g) icing sugar

1. Line an 8″ diameter baking tin.
2. Sift together the flour, sugar, baking powder, bicarbonate of soda, cinnamon and salt. Make a well in the centre, add the eggs, oil and vanilla essence and combine the mixture well.
3. Stir in the carrot, apple, walnuts and sultanas, mix well and pour into the prepared tin.
4. Bake in a pre-heated oven (325°F/170°C, gas mark 3-4) for 1 hour and 20 minutes. Let the cake cool in the tin for 15 minutes, then turn out onto a wire rack and allow to cool completely before topping with the frosting.
5. Make the frosting. Cream together the cheese and margarine and add the icing sugar. Spread the mixture over the cake.

Lavender Biscuits

Heacham, in Norfolk, is famous worldwide as the home of England's only commercial lavender farm, which fills the air for miles around with delightful perfumes in summer. Browse round the National Collection of lavenders or head for the Millers Cottage Tea Room where these unusual, light biscuits seem the natural choice!

8oz (225g) unsalted butter (or 6oz margarine, 2oz butter)
4oz (110g) caster sugar
1 egg, lightly beaten

6oz (175g) Self Raising flour
1 tbsp of dried lavender flowers (crushed)

1. Cream the butter and sugar.
2. Add the egg and beat well.
3. Add the flour, then mix in the lavender flowers.
4. Place teaspoons of the mixture on a baking tray lined with non-stick baking parchment. Bake at 180°C/350°F/gas 4 for approximately 10-15 minutes or until the biscuits are pale golden in colour.

Makes approximately 24 biscuits. These biscuits need careful handling as they are very fragile.

Orange & Apricot Squares

The North Norfolk Heritage Coast is internationally recognised as an important centre for wildlife, with its sand dunes, shingle banks and wide sandy beaches. Halfway along is Holkham Hall, a majestic stately home built in the Palladian style, open to the public. Just beyond the main entrance, The Ancient House Tearoom houses a gallery and gift shop as well as the award-winning tea-rooms managed by Betty Neeve, where this unusual slice is amongst the top sellers.

7oz (200g) chopped, dried apricots
2 tsp. grated orange rind
2 eggs
8½oz (232g) Self Raising flour

4½oz (125g) butter
9oz (250g) soft brown sugar
1 tbsp. orange juice

TOPPING
4½oz (125g) icing sugar
2 tsp. grated orange rind
2oz (50g) chopped walnuts

¾oz (15g) butter
1 tbsp. orange juice

1. Soak apricots in boiling water for about 10 minutes or until soft. Drain well.
2. Grease and line a 25cm x 30cm Swiss roll tin.
3. Cream butter, rind and sugar until light and fluffy, beat in eggs one at a time until well combined.
4. Stir in orange juice and apricots then sifted flour.
5. Spread mixture into tin and bake in a moderate oven (170°C/325°F/gas 3) for about 20 minutes or until brown. Stand for 10 minutes.
6. Make the topping. Sift icing sugar into small heatproof bowl, add butter, rind and orange juice and stir over hot water until icing is smooth and spreadable. Spread over the cake.
7. Sprinkle nuts on top and allow to cool in the tin. Cut into squares and remove from tin.

Norton House Home-made Rock Cakes

The quiet village of Henfield, in West Sussex, is the perfect setting for a summer cricket match on the smooth green. The perfect setting too for the Olde English Teahouse — a charming Grade II listed building, Norton House, run by John and Jean Sinclair Young. Jean bakes all the meringues, biscuits and cakes herself, including her famous rock cakes, made to an old recipe handed down through her family.

8oz (225g) Self Raising flour
4oz (110g) margarine
1oz (25g) sultanas
1oz (25g) currants

1oz (25g) granulated sugar
1 egg
milk to mix

1. Rub the margarine into the flour.
2. Add remaining dry ingredients and mix together.
3. Add the beaten egg and sufficient milk to mix to a soft but stiff consistency.
4. Spoon the mixture onto a greased baking tray in heaps (8-9 rock cakes).
5. Sprinkle a little granulated sugar onto the top of each rock cake before placing them in a hot oven for 20 minutes (200°C/400°F or gas mark 6).

Cherry & Almond Slice

The Courtyard Centre is laid out around a listed Georgian farm complex, a thriving community of craft workshops and country trades. Developed by Mike Wise and his wife Linda, the centre lies just off the Poole by-pass in Dorset, a mile or so from Lytchett Minster. At the heart of the Courtyard is Dylan's Tea Room, where Linda's home cooking attracts a regular stream of visitors. This is one of their favourites — there are threats of World War III when supplies run out!

BASE
6oz (175g) butter or margarine
9oz (250g) plain flour
3oz (75g) caster sugar

4oz (110g) sultanas
5oz (150g) cherries (roughly chopped)

TOPPING
5oz (150g) butter or margarine
5oz (150g) caster sugar
2 eggs
5oz (150g) ground almonds

a few drops of almond essence
3oz (75g) flaked almonds
icing sugar to dust

1. Grease and line a shallow baking tin, and set oven to gas mark 4/350°F/180°C.
2. Cream butter and sugar together and gradually add flour. Mix until fairly firm, turn into prepared tin and press into the bottom evenly with the back of a spoon.
3. Lay sultanas and chopped cherries on the mix.
4. Mix the topping by creaming together the butter and caster sugar, and then add the eggs, mixing well. Add ground almonds and a few drops of almond essence.
5. Spread the mixture over the fruit base and sprinkle with the flaked almonds.
6. Bake in the middle of the oven until golden brown, and firm to the touch.

Sultana Flapjack

Behind the Hillside Cottage Tea Room towers the massive bulk of Lion Rock: in front runs the river backed by the magnificent scenery of Somerset's Cheddar Gorge. The perfect setting to enjoy cream teas and home-made delights such as this delicious Sultana Flapjack.

6oz (175g) margarine　　　　　　*1lb (450g) porridge oats*
4½oz (125g) clear honey　　　　　*2½oz (60g) sultanas*

1. Pre-heat oven to 180°C (350°F), gas mark 4.
2. Heat margarine and honey in a saucepan until melted. Stir in the sultanas and oats, mixing thoroughly.
3. Turn into a greased 7 x 11 inch baking tray, spreading evenly. Bake for 20 minutes.
4. When cool, cut into twelve bars. Remove from tray and store in an airtight container.

Fudge Chocolate Cake

At Fables tea-room and antique shop in Malmesbury, Wiltshire, proprietor Jill Eatwell serves an appetising selection of home-baked delights. This gooey concoction is particularly popular.

3½tbsp cocoa powder　　　　　　*8oz (225g) self-raising flour*
4oz (110g) butter　　　　　　　　*2 eggs, beaten*
4fl oz (110ml) oil　　　　　　　　*4fl oz (110ml) milk*
8fl oz (275ml) water　　　　　　　*½tsp bicarbonate of soda*
12oz (350g) caster sugar　　　　　*1tsp vanilla essence*

ICING
3½tbsp cocoa powder　　　　　　*1lb (450g) icing sugar, sifted*
4oz (110g) butter　　　　　　　　*1tsp vanilla essence*
3oz (75g) evaporated milk

1. Thoroughly grease and fully line a 2lb loaf tin, greasing the paper lining too.
2. Place the cocoa , butter, oil and water in a pan and bring to the boil.
3. Remove from the heat and stir in the sugar and flour.
4. Beat the eggs, milk, soda and essence together and add to the rest of the mixture. Turn into the prepared tin and bake at gas mark 4/180°C/350°F for 1¼-1½ hours. Turn out onto a wire rack to cool.
5. Make the icing. Bring all the ingredients to the boil, beat until smooth and pour over cake while it is still warm. Smooth out.

Caraway Seed Cake

The Victorian charm of Royal Leamington Spa is echoed in Sue Gallagher's wonderful recreation of a gracious 19th-century tea-room, Jephson's, overlooking The Parade. This traditional recipe is delightful with Afternoon Tea.

8oz (225g) self-raising flour　　　*1tsp baking powder*
6oz (175g) butter　　　　　　　　*1 tbsp cold water*
5oz (150g) sugar　　　　　　　　*2 tbsp caraway seeds*
2 eggs

1. Pre-heat the oven to 180°C/350°F/gas mark 4.
2. Beat the butter and sugar to a cream, adding the eggs one at a time.
3. Stir in the flour and baking powder and add the caraway seeds.
4. Bake in a greased, lined cake tin for 1½ hours.

Barton Chocolate Bar

The Sea Cottage Tea Shoppe stands looking out over the waves at Barton on Sea, near New Milton in Hampshire. Kevin Noon and Wendy Bromfield receive many visitors here, who love to chat about recipes. This recipe was given by a Canadian visitor who described it as "an absolutely decadent cake". Adapted by Wendy, it features regularly on the loaded cake trolley, a great favourite with all the customers.

LAYER 1

4oz (110g) butter	*1 tbsp. cocoa*
2oz (50g) sugar	*8oz (225g) biscuit crumbs*
1 egg	*2oz (50g) dessicated coconut*
1 tsp. vanilla	*2oz (50g) chopped nuts*

LAYER 2

4oz (110g) butter	*8oz (225g) icing sugar*
3 tbsp. milk	*2 tbsp. custard powder*

LAYER 3

5oz (150g) semi sweet chocolate	*1 tbsp. butter*

1. Make layer 1. Mix the butter, sugar, egg, vanilla and cocoa over boiling water until slightly thickened (use a double saucepan for layers 1 and 3). Then mix in the biscuit crumbs, coconut and nuts. Put in a 9″ square greased tin and press down so base is evenly spread. Stand in fridge for 15 minutes.
2. Make layer 2. Beat together butter, milk, icing sugar and custard powder until creamy and spread over layer 1. Stand in fridge for 15 minutes.
3. Melt chocolate and butter over hot (not boiling) water and spread over layer 2.
4. Allow to set in fridge. Cut into squares.

Norfolk Shortcakes

On the corner of Church Street and White Lion Street in Holt, Norfolk, are the tea-rooms known to everyone as "The Owl", run by Dawn and Terry Hulbert. Not just tea-rooms but a bake shop too — almost everything produced in The Owl's kitchens, from quiches and pies to cakes and preserves. These shortcakes are baked fresh every day, a traditional item on the Owl menu.

1lb (450g) shortcrust pastry	*sultanas*
sugar	*butter or margarine*

1. Roll out the shortcrust pastry.
2. Sprinkle with sugar, sultanas and dobs of butter or margarine.
3. Fold ⅓ of the pastry onto itself and then fold over the other ⅓.
4. Roll out again and cut into squares.
5. Place on a lightly greased baking tray and bake at 200°C/400°F/gas 6 for approximately 15 minutes or until golden brown.

Chocolate Brownies

The charming medieval village of Dunster, in Somerset, boasts an equally charming Water Mill — a fully working operation which produces some 30 tons of wholewheat flour a year. Some of it finds its way into Marcia Marriott's delectable breads and cakes, served in the Mill's own tea-room, such as these rich chocolate squares — Marcia's speciality!

2oz (50g) Dunster Mill wholewheat flour
1oz (25g) cocoa
½ level tsp baking powder
4oz (110g) butter

8oz (225g) dark soft brown sugar
2 eggs
1 tsp vanilla essence
4oz (110g) chopped walnuts
1 tbsp milk

TOPPING
3oz (75g) plain chocolate
2 tbsp milk
1oz (25g) butter

1 tsp instant coffee
1 tbsp boiling water
6oz (175g) icing sugar

1. Grease a 10" x 6" shallow tin and line the base with greaseproof paper.
2. Cream the fat and sugar, beat in the eggs and vanilla essence.
3. Add the dry ingredients and milk.
4. Place in the lined tin and bake at 160°C/312°F/gas 2½ for 35 minutes. Leave to cool.
5. Make the topping. Melt the chocolate, add the milk, fat and coffee dissolved in the boiling water. Beat in icing sugar. Spread mixture evenly over the cooked sponge. When set, cut into squares.

Frome Fairings

Perched on the eastern end of the Mendip Hills, the old market town of Frome with its steep, narrow lanes is a fascinating place to explore. Fascinating too is the Settle tea-shop in Cheap Street run by Margaret Vaughan, familiar to many as the presenter of her own TV series "Fruity Passions". These spicy biscuits are cooked and eaten when the fair comes to town but are delicious at any time of year!

4oz (110g) self raising flour
pinch of salt
¼tsp ground ginger
¼tsp mixed spice
¼tsp cinnamon

1½tsp bicarbonate of soda
2oz (50g) butter
2oz (50g) caster sugar
1½ level dessertspn golden syrup

1. Pre-heat the oven to 375°F/190°C/gas mark 5.
2. Sift the flour, salt, ground ginger, cinnamon and mixed spice and bicarbonate of soda into a basin.
3. Rub the butter into the dry ingredients. Mix in the sugar. Melt the syrup and stir it into the mixture, to make a soft dough.
4. Roll the mixture between the hands into balls about the size of marbles and place them on greased baking trays with a space between them to allow them to spread. Place in the oven for 10-15 minutes.
5. Take the fairings out of the oven and hit the tins on a solid surface to make the fairings crack and spread. Then put them back into the oven for another five minutes to finish baking. Place in the oven for 10-15 minutes.

Sticky Gingerbread

The pretty East Sussex village of East Hoathly is home to Clara's Coffee Shop, where home-baking is very much the order of the day. Here is just one of the sticky delights on offer.

4oz (110g) margarine
6oz (175g) black treacle
2oz (50g) golden syrup
¼ pint (150ml) milk
8oz (225g) plain flour

2oz (50g) brown sugar
1 level tsp mixed spice
1 level tsp bicarbonate soda
1-2 level tsp ground ginger
2 eggs

1. Gently melt the margarine, black treacle, syrup and sugar.
2. Add the milk and allow to cool.
3. Sieve the dry ingredients together into a bowl and add the treacle mixture with the eggs and beat together.
4. Pour into a well greased tin (preferably a square one) and bake for 1-1½ hours at 150°C/300°F/gas 2. *Makes 9 generous squares.*

Banana Cake

From Whalebone House in the pretty Norfolk coastal village of Cley-next-the-Sea comes this moist, tangy cake that really melts in the mouth. Relax to the strains of classical music and sample Stuart and Selina Bragg's delicious home-cooking.

8oz (225g) Self Raising flour
6oz (175g) caster sugar
4oz (110g) margarine
pinch of salt
½ tsp mixed spice

1lb (450g) mashed ripe bananas
4oz (110g) mixed dried fruit
2oz (50g) walnuts, chopped
2 eggs, beaten

1. Sieve the flour, spice and salt into a large bowl and rub in the margarine.
2. Add remaining ingredients and mix well.
3. Pour into a greased and lined 2lb loaf tin.
4. Bake at 180°C/350°F/gas 4 for 1 hour 10 minutes until golden brown.
5. When cool, decorate with a small amount of glacé icing made with lemon juice and sprinkle with grated orange rind.

Coconut Cake

Just north of Bury St. Edmunds, the village of Great Barton is home to "Craft at the Suffolk Barn", where Margaret and Geoffrey Ellis welcome visitors to their wild flower garden, craft shop and tea-room. This light, fluffy cake with a crisp meringue topping, is just one of Margaret's delicious creations, often served in the tea-room.

4oz (110g) Self Raising flour
6oz (175g) margarine
1 tsp baking powder
3oz (75g) golden syrup

4oz (110g) dessicated coconut
2 egg yolks
4oz (110g) castor sugar

TOPPING
2 egg whites
1 tsp vanilla essence

2oz (50g) castor sugar

1. Line a shallow baking tray (9 x 11 or 12 x 8 inches) with non-stick paper.
2. Blend all the ingredients for the cake together and pour into the tray.
3. Make the topping. Whisk egg whites until they are stiff, add sugar and vanilla essence and spread evenly over cake mixture.
4. Cook immediately in a moderate oven (350°F/180°C/gas 4) for about 40 minutes, or until the meringue is crisp. Cut into slices when cold.

Apricot Slices

It would be a brave man who singled out one particular village as the loveliest in the Cotswolds, but everyone (almost!) accepts Painswick's claim to be "Queen of the Cotswolds". A few steps away from the church is St. Michael's Restaurant, a charming stone cottage where Pat and Bryan Mansfield provide an unbeatable combination of fresh, tasty food and friendly service. This rich fruity shortbread is one of Pat's favourites — it sells "like hot cakes"!

FOR THE SHORTBREAD

12oz (350g) soft margarine
6oz (175g) caster sugar

18oz (500g) plain flour

FOR THE FILLING

8oz (225g) dried apricots
8oz (225g) stoned dates

2 large cooking apples, peeled and cored
breakfast orange juice

1. Line a 9" x 12" meat tin with bakewell paper.
2. Mix all the shortbread ingredients together until they resemble breadcrumbs.
3. Put almost half of the mixture in the bottom of the lined tin and pat flat.
4. In a saucepan, place chopped dates, apricots and cooking apples and pour over sufficient orange juice to cover. Cook slowly on a low heat until quite mushy, then leave to go cold.
5. Spread the cooled fruit mixture over the shortbread.
6. Cover with remaining shortbread and pat down. Generously sprinkle top with caster sugar.
7. Place in oven and bake at 180°C/350°F/gas mark 4 until pale golden in colour.
8. Leave to cool, cut into slices and serve.

Caribbean Fruit Cake

To the east of Stowmarket in Suffolk, at Stonham Parva, an intriguing arch spans the A140 road, a landmark throughout the area. Nearby, Cora Pullen runs the Whistling Mouse Crafts and Tea Room, where this moist "tropical" fruit cake is always a great favourite. As an alternative, the pineapple can be replaced by a small tin of apricots, drained and chopped.

8oz (225g) Self Raising flour
6oz (175g) soft brown sugar
6oz (175g) sunflower margarine
2 large eggs, beaten

8oz (225g) mixed, dried fruit
8oz (225g) can crushed pineapple (well drained)

1. Cream the margarine and sugar together, add the eggs and beat well.
2. Add the flour, dried fruit and pineapple and mix very well.
3. Put into a greased, lined 8" deep cake tin and bake for 1½-1¾ hours at 160°C/310°F/gas 2½ until nicely browned and an inserted metal skewer comes out clean.
4. Leave in tin for about 10 minutes, then turn out onto a wire tray to cool.

Orange Chocolate Drizzle Cake

The pleasant little town of Warminster, in Wiltshire, is home to Rosie's Tea Shop, set down a little alleyway just off the Market Place. Owners Sally Petrie and Jean Blackwell are renowned for their delicious home-baked fare, including this tangy and unusual cake which is always very popular with customers.

FOR THE CAKE
6oz (175g) margarine
6oz (175g) caster sugar
6oz (175g) self raising flour
3 eggs
2oz (50g) chocolate drops
2tbsp cold milk
finely grated rind of 2 oranges

FOR THE ORANGE TOPPING
juice of 2 oranges
4oz (110g) caster sugar

CHOCOLATE TOPPING
4oz (110g) plain chocolate cake covering   *½oz (10g) butter*

1. Pre-heat the oven to 350°F/180°C/gas mark 4 and grease and line a 2lb (910g) loaf tin.
2. Cream the margarine and sugar together until pale and creamy. Beat in the eggs, one at a time, alternating with the flour.
3. Add the milk, chocolate drops and orange rind and mix thoroughly.
4. Put the mixture into the prepared tin and bake in the pre-heated oven for 1 hour. When cooked, turn out onto a wire rack to cool.
5. While the cake is cooking, "soak" the caster sugar in the orange juice. When the cake is almost cold, cut slits in the top and "drizzle" the orange syrup across it. Top the cake with melted butter and chocolate mixture and leave to set. Cut into 8-10 slices.

Dorset Apple Cake

Apples feature in many traditional Dorset dishes — both sweet and savoury. The story goes that a young girl would place an apple pip on the fire to test her sweetheart's true feelings. If the pip burst with the heat, she knew he loved her. If it simply burnt, he did not. Hence the rhyme,

> *"If you love me, pop and fly,*
> *If you hate me, lay and die."*

Merry Bolton uses this popular fruit in her version of Dorset Apple Cake, a firm favourite at the delightful Cliff Cottage Tea Garden in Lyme Regis, Dorset, with its spectacular views out over the sea.

8oz (225g) peeled, cored and chopped apples
4oz (110g) margarine
1½ tsps baking powder
8oz (225g) plain flour
4oz (110g) sugar
1 egg and a little milk
1 pinch salt
1 tsp ginger
1tsp cinnamon

1. Place the flour, salt and spices in a bowl and rub in the fat.
2. Add the baking powder and sugar.
3. Make a firmish dough by adding the egg and milk and stirring well.
4. Stir in the apples, pour into a greased cake tin and bake in a moderate oven (350°F/180°C/gas 4) for 45-50 minutes.
5. Serve warm or cold with lots of clotted cream!

Bienenstick

The National Trust village of Lacock in Wiltshire is full of history and charm. This is where you'll find the 13th-century King John's Hunting Lodge, home of Robert and Jane Woods, who serve delicious scones and cakes in their beamed tea-room by a blazing log fire.

FOR THE CAKE

7oz (200g) Quark
14oz (400g) self-raising flour
3oz (75g) caster sugar

1 heaped tsp baking powder
¼pt (150ml) sunflower oil
¼pt (150ml) milk

FOR THE CUSTARD FILLING

1 egg
1 egg white
3oz (75g) caster sugar

1tsp arrowroot
½pt (275ml) milk
vanilla essence

FOR THE TOPPING

2oz (50g) flaked almonds
3½-4oz (100g) honey

a little water

1. Make the custard filling. Mix together the egg, egg white, sugar and arrowroot in a saucepan. Add the milk and a few drops of vanilla essence and heat gently, beating all the time with a ballon whisk, until the mixture has thickened. Remove from the heat and allow to cool.
2. Make the cake mixture. Blend the Quark, oil and milk to a smooth paste. Add the flour, sugar and baking powder and blend to form a smooth dough.
3. Divide into two equal portions. Flatten out into greased, lined 11 inch flan tins as though making a pizza base, with slightly raised edges. (Hint: oil hands with sunflower oil to stop dough sticking). Bake at 200°C/400°F/gas mark 6 until risen, but not brown.
4. Meanwhile make the topping. In a heavy saucepan, gently heat the honey, water and almonds until the mixture is just beginning to darken.
5. Pour onto the top of one of the cakes and spread evenly over. Return both halves to the oven and bake till golden brown. Remove from the oven and cool.
6. Assemble the cake. Place the plain cake top-side down and spread the custard filling evenly over the top. Place the honey and almond-coated cake on top, honey-side up.

NB. This cake can be made egg-free by substituting puréed apricot for the custard filling.

Boiled Fruit Cake

The village of Abbotsbury is as pretty as Dorset can offer. In its centre (opposite the Ilchester Arms) is The Old Schoolhouse gift shop and tea room run by Sally and Chris Dawson, where this brandy boiled fruit cake goes down a treat.

8oz (225g) margarine
12oz (350g) granulated sugar
1½lb (700g) mixed dried fruit
½pt (275ml) water
2 level tsp bicarbonate of soda

2 heaped tsp mixed spice
4 beaten eggs
1lb (450g) plain flour
large pinch of salt
2 x tots of brandy

1. Place the margarine, sugar, fruit, water, bicarbonate of soda and mixed spice in a saucepan.
2. Bring to the boil and simmer for 1 minute.
3. Pour into a large bowl and allow to cool, then add 2 measures of brandy.
4. Line a 9″ cake tin.
5. Add the eggs, flour and salt to the cooled mixture and mix well. Pour into the prepared cake tin.
6. Bake in the centre of the oven for 1¼ hours at 180°C/350°F/gas mark 4.

Christmas Pudding

Bartley Mill near Frant in Sussex is renowned for its stone ground organic flours and quality wholefood products. This unusual version of a traditional favourite, created by Gail Duff, will go down a treat on Christmas Day!

4oz (125g) currants
4oz (125g) raisins
4oz (125g) sultanas
2oz (50g) candied peel, preferably in one piece
2oz (50g) stoned dates
¼ pint (150ml) Guinness or Beamish stout
1oz (25g) almonds
1 small Bramley apple
1 medium carrot

1½oz (40g) wholemeal flour
1½oz (40g) wholemeal breadcrumbs
2oz (50g) beef suet, finely grated if fresh, or the packet kind as it is
½ tsp baking powder
pinch fine sea salt
¼ nutmeg, grated
½ tsp ground cinnamon
1 egg, beaten
4 tbs brandy
butter for greasing

1. Put the currants, raisins and sultanas into a bowl. Finely chop the candied peel and the dates. Put them into a bowl with the others. Mix in 4 fl oz (125ml) stout. Cover and leave for 24 hours.
2. Blanch and shred the almonds. Grate the apple and carrot. Mix these into the soaked fruit.
3. Put the flour and breadcrumbs into a mixing bowl. Add the suet, baking powder, salt and spices. Mix in the fruit plus all its liquid, the egg, remaining stout and brandy. Stir well and have a wish!
4. Butter a 1½ pint (850ml) pudding basin. Put in the mixture, press it down and smooth the top. Cut a ring of greaseproof paper and one of foil. Grease the paper. Lay it, greased side down over the basin. Put the foil on top. Tie them down with string making a handle for lifting. Trim them neatly to make a frill about 1 inch (2.5cm) wide.
5. Bring a large pan of water to the boil. The water must not come over the bottom of the frill. Lower in the pudding. Cover and steam it for 4 hours, topping up the water as and when necessary. Lift out the pudding, cool it and replace the foil and greaseproof.

This type of pudding, without sugar, will not keep for a long time. It can be stored in the refrigerator for up to three weeks.
On Christmas morning, steam the pudding for a further 2 hours. *Serves 8.*

Eighteenth-Century Lemon Cheese Cake

Four miles west of Droitwich Spa in Worcestershire, the village of Ombersley glories in some remarkable architecture. One of the oldest buildings, the Priest's House (1269), is home to The Ombersley Gallery and Tea Room, where Carole Pimm has gained a formidable reputation for her imaginative home cooking. This unusual, tangy cheese cake is always a popular choice.

1 Sweet Pastry Case

LEMON CHEESE
4oz/(110g) butter
4oz/(110g) sugar
4 egg yolks
zest and juice of 4 lemons

FILLING
6oz/(175g) sugar
6oz/(175g) butter
4oz/(110g) breadcrumbs
3 large eggs
zest and juice of 4 lemons

1. Make pastry case — bake blind in 8″ tin dish.
2. Lemon Cheese — whisk together butter, sugar, egg yolks and lemon zest and juice in a bowl over boiling water until thick (N.B. This is a very slow process).
3. Filling — beat together sugar and butter until white, add breadcrumbs, eggs and lemon zest and juice.
4. Make up the tart. Smooth a good layer of lemon cheese over the base of the flan and then fill to the top with lemon filling.
5. Bake at 200°C, 400°F, gas 6 for approx. 30 minutes. Ideally the cheesecake is best served still a little warm with icing sugar dredged over it.

Caribbean Bakewell

Henley-in-Arden, near Warwick, is known for its mile-long High Street lined with a picturesque jumble of ancient houses, shops and inns. Here too you'll find Hazel's tea-room, where Hazel Halliday's inventive and constantly changing menu brings back customers time and time again.

8oz (225g) short crust pastry

FILLING
4oz (110g) margarine
4oz (110g) caster sugar
2 eggs (lightly beaten)
2oz (50g) ground almonds
2oz (50g) self raising flour
few drops of almond essence
4 tbsp pineapple jam

2 small bananas
rind of ½ lemon
rind of ½ orange
3 pineapple rings in natural juice, drained
dessicated coconut or flaked almonds to decorate

1. Roll out the short crust pastry and line eight 4″ patty tins or one 9″ flan dish (approx. 1-1½″ deep).
2. Spread pineapple jam over the bottom of the cases and arrange slices of pineapple and banana on the jam.
3. Cream the butter and sugar together, add the eggs and beat well. Add the remaining filling ingredients and mix to a soft consistency.
4. Put the filling mixture in the pastry cases on top of the fruit and jam and sprinkle with either a little coconut or flaked almonds. Bake in the oven for 30 minutes at 180°C/350°F/gas mark 4. Turn out and cool on a wire rack.

French Apple Flan

In the heart of the Suffolk countryside, off the B1084 near Woodbridge, you will find The Butley Pottery and Teashop. Honor Hussey's majolica ware bowls and platters are not the only attraction here. The old stables have been converted into a delightful tea-room, where this delicious flan is a great favourite with Honor's many "regulars".

8oz (225g) plain flour
4oz (110g) castor sugar
4oz (110g) butter
4 egg yolks

1-2 cooking apples
1 tbsp raspberry jam
1½ tbsp hot water

1. Place flour, sugar and butter on a clean work surface. Make a well in the centre and add egg yolks.
2. Work all ingredients together until they form a firm dough. Wrap dough in a polythene bag and leave in refrigerator for at least ½ hour.
3. Grease an 8″ flan tin; press dough into tin with fingers until spread evenly over the base and slightly raised at the edges.
4. Peel and core the apples; slice very thinly and arrange neatly on top of the dough.
5. Melt jam with hot water and spoon over the apples, completely coating them.
6. Bake in a moderate oven (180°C/350°F/gas 4) for approximately 30 minutes until dough and apples are nicely browned.
7. Serve hot or cold — with cream for a treat!

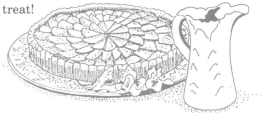

Apricot & Maple Syrup Pudding

The Olde Bakery Tea Shoppe in Winchcombe, Gloucestershire, closed as a bakery 20 years ago. Yet the tradition of home-baking has been maintained by Colin and Sally Snell who have concocted this delicious, warming pud for their visitors.

2 tbsp maple syrup
14oz can of apricot halves (drained)
4oz (110g) margarine
4oz (110g) caster sugar

2 eggs
Few drops of vanilla essence
6oz (175g) Self Raising flour

1. Oil a 2 pint pudding basin. Pour the maple syrup into the base and arrange apricot halves in the bottom.
2. In a bowl mix together the margarine, sugar, eggs, vanilla essence and flour and place on top of the apricots. Cover the basin with greaseproof paper or foil and tie in place with fine string.
3. Steam for about 1½ hours in the traditional way, over simmering hot water, topping up the water if necessary.
4. When cooked, turn out onto a serving plate and serve with custard, cream or ice cream.

NOTE: This pudding may be cooked in a microwave oven. The only difference in this case is that the maple syrup should NOT be put in the bottom of the basin. Otherwise prepare the pudding as above and cook on full power (700 watt) for 6 minutes and then allow to stand for 2 minutes. Turn out onto a serving plate and then pour the maple syrup over the top.

Bread Pudding

The exquisite village of Eardisland, with its timbered houses and pretty gardens, is set on the banks of the River Arrow in Herefordshire. The perfect setting for the Eardisland Tea Room and Gift Shop run by Barry and Kathleen Freeman, whose bread pudding is always a popular treat.

5 or 6 pieces of stale bread
milk
4-5oz (110-150g) mixed dried fruit

1oz (25g) crystalised ginger (optional)
1 heaped tsp mixed spice
2oz (50g) demerara sugar

1. Break the bread up into fine crumbs in an electric mixer if you have one.
2. Add the mixed dried fruit (including chopped up pieces of ginger if liked) and the spice and sugar. Mix all the dry ingredients together and add enough milk to absorb into them.
3. Place the mixture into a well greased basin or pyrex dish which has first been sprinkled liberally with demerara sugar. Dot the top with tiny pieces of margarine. Bake for 30 minutes at 375°F/190°C/gas mark 5.

The above ingredients are approximate only and can be adapted to suit personal tastes. Bread pudding is best eaten the day it is made and is delicious served hot with either cream or ice cream.

NB: This recipe may be microwaved and will take about 15 minutes.

Fruit Tartlet

One of the most popular villages on the Isle of Wight, Godshill boasts a magnificent 14th century hilltop church surrounded by enchanting thatched cottages. You'll also find the Old Smithy with its model of the whole island, a wonderfully scented herb garden and gift and fashion shop. This is just one of the tasty treats on offer in the spacious, elegant tea-rooms.

PASTRY
8oz (225g) plain flour
5oz (150g) margarine

2oz (50g) sugar
1 egg

PASTRY CREAM
2 egg yolks
2oz (50g) caster sugar
1oz (25g) flour

½ pint (300ml) milk
vanilla essence to taste
fruit of your choice

1. To make the pastry, rub fat into flour until it resembles fine breadcrumbs. Stir in sugar.
2. Add egg and mix until it forms a dough.
3. Chill for 30 minutes then roll out to line a loose-bottomed flan ring.
4. Bake blind for 25-30 minutes at 220°C/425°F/gas mark 7.
5. Make the pastry cream. Boil milk in thick-bottomed pan.
6. Cream sugar and egg yolks together, add flour and add the boiled milk.
7. Clean pan, then bring liquid back to boil stirring all the time. Add essence to taste. Pour into cooked flan.
8. Decorate with fruit of your choice. Coat with glaze made from sieved jam and water.

Old Thatch Carrot Cake

Shanklin Old Village, on the Isle of Wight, was once a thriving fishing village. Today it features on hundreds of postcards and chocolate boxes with its picturesque thatched cottages and pretty gardens. One such cottage now houses the Old Thatch Tea-Room run by Kathy and Frederick Pink, where this delicious moist carrot cake goes down a treat.

4oz (110g) plain flour, sieved   4oz (110g) grated carrot
1 tsp. baking powder   2 eggs, beaten
8oz (225g) sugar   5oz oil

1. Put all ingredients in a food processor or mixer or mix well by hand.
2. Turn into a greased and lined tin and bake at gas 4/350°F/180°C for one hour.
3. Turn out and allow to cool. Meanwhile make the topping.

TOPPING
4oz (110g) cream cheese   4-6oz (110-175g) icing sugar
2oz (50g) butter   1 tsp. vanilla essence

Whisk all ingredients together until smooth and creamy and spread onto the cold cake.

Butterscotch Meringue Pie

The quaint town of Ellesmere in the heart of the "Shropshire lakes", holds some delightful surprises. Not least is Nightingales, just off the Square in Market Street, where Ian and Susan Fullard have established a warm, friendly environment and a reputation for fine, home-made food. The only problem with this delicious Butterscotch Meringue is that one portion is never enough!

SHORTCRUST PASTRY
8oz (250g) plain flour   1oz/25g lard
3oz/75g butter   water or milk to bind

FILLING AND TOPPING
8oz (250g) light brown sugar   1 tsp vanilla essence
2oz (50g) plain flour   salt
8 fl oz (250ml) milk   pinch of cream of tartar
4 large eggs, separated   2 oz (50g) caster sugar
1 tbsp butter, cut into pieces

1. Make the pastry. Rub butter and lard into the flour and add enough milk or water to bind. Rest the dough for ½ hour in the fridge before use.
2. On a lightly floured surface, roll out the dough to about ⅛" thickness and fit into a 9" (23cm) pie plate. Crimp the edges with your fingers, prick the bottom with a fork and chill for ½ hour. Line with greaseproof paper, fill with uncooked rice and bake in a hot oven (220°C, 425°F, gas 7) for 15 minutes. Remove paper and rice and bake for a further 10 minutes until golden. Place on a rack to cool.
3. In a saucepan, mix together the brown sugar and flour. Whisk in 2 fl. oz./50ml of water and the milk. Simmer over a low heat for 5 minutes or until the mixture is smooth.
4. Remove from the heat and whisk in the egg yolks, one at a time, then the butter and vanilla essence. Cool slightly and pour into the pastry case.
5. In a bowl, whisk the egg whites with a pinch of salt and cream of tartar until stiff. Pipe or spoon onto the filling, covering it completely. Dredge with caster sugar.
6. Bake in a pre-heated, slow oven (150°C, 300°F, gas 2) for 20 minutes until golden brown.
7. Serve by itself, or with cream or ice cream.

Mrs Jones' Rich Rice Pudding

From Shropshire's historic Ironbridge Gorge Museum comes this traditional, creamy pudding recipe, which goes down a treat on cold winter days!

4oz (110g) short-grain rice	3 eggs
1½ pints (845ml) milk	1 tsp. mixed spice
2oz (50g) butter	grated rind of half a lemon or 1 tsp. of
3oz (75g) caster sugar	lemon juice

1. Pre-heat oven to gas mark 2, 300°F (150°C) and butter a 2 pint baking dish.
2. Put rice into a saucepan, add the milk and bring slowly almost to simmering point, then let it cook very gently until the rice is practically tender, which should take about 10 minutes.
3. Add the sugar and butter and stir until they have dissolved and melted.
4. Now take the saucepan off the heat and let the mixture cool a little, then stir in the eggs — well beaten — with the lemon. Pour the mixture into the baking dish, sprinkle with mixed spice and bake for 30-40 minutes (or longer if you like it really thick). Serve with pouring cream.   *Serves 4.*

Hungarian Nut Torte

Notcutts Garden Centres at Solihull near Birmingham and Nuneham Courtenay near Oxford are just two of a string of top quality horticultural establishments dotted around the south of England. This unusual dessert is just one of the home-cooked varieties on offer in the Terrace Restaurant.

FOR THE HAZELNUT BASE

4oz (110g) unblanched hazelnuts	5oz (150g) caster sugar
4 eggs	

FOR THE FILLING

2oz (50g) unsalted butter	1 heaped dessertspn cocoa powder
2oz (50g) icing sugar	1 heaped tsp instant coffee

FOR THE TOPPING

3oz (75g) caster sugar	12 hazelnuts

1. Pre-heat the oven to 180°C/350°F/gas mark 4 and grease two x 7 inch sandwich tins.
2. Place the hazelnuts in a liquidiser and grind finely.
3. Separate the eggs and beat the whites until they are stiff.
4. Whisk the yolks with 5oz of caster sugar until they are pale and creamy.
5. Fold quantities of the nuts and egg whites alternately into the egg yolk mixture. Divide this mixture between the two greased sandwich tins and bake in the middle of the pre-heated oven for 30 minutes. To test if the cakes are completely cooked, when the tops are lightly pressed with a finger no impression should be left.
6. When cooked, remove from the oven and allow to cool slightly before turning out onto a wire rack.
7. Make the filling. Cream the butter until it is very soft and fluffy. Add the icing sugar, continue to beat slowly and incorporate the cocoa powder and coffee.
8. When the cakes are cold, sandwich them together with the filling.
9. Make the topping. Place three dessertspoons of water in a heavy-based saucepan along with the remaining caster sugar (3oz). Stir over a low heat until the sugar has dissolved, then boil the mixture rapidly. When it is a rich golden colour immediately pour it over the top of the cake. With a slightly oiled knife, spread the caramel over the cake and decorate with the 12 hazelnuts.